Christians are for ever!

Christians are for ever!

An easier-to-read and abridged version of
the classic "The Doctrine of the
Saints' Perseverance Explained and
Confirmed", by John Owen

Prepared by H. Lawrence

Joint Managing Editors
J. P. Arthur, M.A.
H. J. Appleby

© GRACE PUBLICATIONS TRUST
139 Grosvenor Avenue
London, N5 2NH,
England.

1987

Reprinted 1996

ISBN 0 946462 14 3

Distributed by: EVANGELICAL PRESS
12 Wooler Street
Darlington
Co. Durham, DL1 1RQ
England

Cover Design: Lawrence Littleton Evans

Typeset by Berea Press, Glasgow
Printed in Great Britain by
Cox & Wyman, Reading.

Contents

*This is chapter 17 in Owen's work. Chapters 11-16 of Owen are omitted here, since they are specifically concerned with a controversy of his day and therefore not so relevant to us.– Ed.

1.
The truth stated

Very different views are held of the doctrine of the perseverance of saints. To some, the strong hope and encouragement which God gives to his people (Hebrews 6:17,18) are based on it. To others, the doctrine forms no part of gospel teaching and is only an invention of men. They see it, even, as a powerful encouragement to sin. A right understanding of this doctrine is, therefore, of great importance. It will influence our walk with God. The glory of God, the honour of the Lord Jesus Christ, and the welfare of the souls of believers are bound up with it.

The fact that many who claim to be Christians fall away from the faith has always been an obstacle to God's people. Jesus foretold that some professing Christians would fall away (Matthew 24:11,12). He comforted his disciples by assuring them that, nevertheless, God's elect would not be deceived or fall away. The apostle Paul spoke of the apostasy, in his time, of Hymenaeus and Philetus. The faith of those who followed their evil teaching was destroyed. But there is a solid foundation for the comfort of true believers – "The Lord knows those who are his" (II Timothy 2:19). The apostle John wrote similarly about the anti-Christs and apostates of his time. "They went out from us," he said, "but they did not really belong to us" (I John 2:19). The fact that some give up the ways of the Lord ought not to shake the faith of true believers. Nevertheless, it should cause them to examine themselves to know whether Christ is in them or not. "If you think you are standing firm, be careful that you don't fall" (I Corinthians 10:12).

Some have argued this way: "If you insist that those who fall away to perdition never were true believers, no-one can be sure whether he has a true faith or not". In answer we may say that God tests believers by these instances. Through such testings they grow in grace and are strengthened in their faith. By the grace of our faithful God we shall be more than conquerors (Romans 8:37). Here we can surely rest. The falling away of some should never be allowed to rob us of that inexpressible and glorious joy in believing which was so evident in the early Christians (I Peter 1:8).

It has been claimed that the only ground of assurance is the testimony of a man's own heart that he is walking uprightly with God. Certainly many believers receive the Spirit of adoption by which the Holy Spirit bears witness with our spirits that we are the children of God (Romans 8:16). Other Christians never reach that full joy in believing which the early church knew. The assurance of our salvation needs to be built on a firmer foundation than even the testimony of our conscience. Such testimony is often weakened by our own failures.

What do we mean by the word "saints"? We could simply say "holy ones", but the word "holy" is used in the scriptures in several senses. In his essential being only God is the "Holy One". The holiness of created beings is different from God's holiness. Adam, when he was created, had an original holiness but lost it by sin.

So had the angels that fell. True believers have holiness given to them even though they have sinned and come short of the glory of God. This is "imparted" holiness.

In the Old Testament especially, the word "holy" often has the meaning: "separated to God and his service". Not only are sacred articles like the ark said to be holy, but also the whole people of Israel, even though there were wicked persons among them. Perseverance is not claimed for these. In the New Testament the word "holy" is more often used to mean "having an inward purity". There are many who think of themselves as holy, or who are thought to be so by others, who were never truly converted. In others the gift of common grace by the Spirit so affects their conduct that they seem to have been born again though Christ does not live in them.

How then are the saints, or true believers, to be distinguished?
1. Though they were once spiritually dead, God has given them faith which brings salvation. Their holiness is the result of God's eternal purpose in their election by his grace (Ephesians 1:4).
2. The Holy Spirit has raised them from their death in sin to newness of life. They obtain the precious gift of faith through the work of the Spirit when they are made alive with Christ (Ephesians 2:5).
3. The Holy Spirit is given in order that he may stay with them for ever (John 14:16) because of the death and intercession of Christ.
4. By reason of the Spirit's work in them they cease to be God's enemies and become his loving and obedient people.

The Holy Spirit uses many expressions to illustrate what perseverance is. Examples are:

1. to walk with Christ as we have received him (Colossians 2:6);
2. to be faithful to death (Revelation 2:10);
3. to hold fast our confidence and faith to the end (Hebrews 3:6);
4. to be kept by the power of God through faith unto salvation (I Peter 1:5).

Let us examine the claim which is sometimes made that believers may completely fall away. Everyone agrees that believers have the Holy Spirit in them and that they bring forth the fruit of the Spirit (Galatians 5:22). If this is so, what could possibly cause believers to lose the Holy Spirit totally? What could cause the utter failure of the outworking of his grace in them? Could sin? Certainly sin, if cherished, will weaken our ability to live the Christian life. The Holy Spirit is provoked and grieved by sin in the believer but it is unthinkable that sin should prove victorious over the Spirit. The grace which believers have results from their being new creatures in Christ Jesus. It is not obtained by their own efforts. The root is first made good and then the fruit is good. Grace is planted in them by that same mighty power which God showed when he raised Jesus Christ from the dead (Ephesians 1:19,20). Continuance in sin on our part certainly deserves that God should take away his Spirit and grace from us, but will our heavenly Father allow sin to have the final victory over his sons and daughters? Will he not rather come to their aid? He may chastise them but he will not cast them away for ever.

It has often been argued by those who oppose the doctrine of the perseverance of saints that such teaching encourages people to sin. They say that it assures people of the love of God and of salvation itself, no matter how sinful their lives may be. This is quite false. Believers who have tasted the love and pardoning mercy of God value it above all the world. They want to do the good things which God has prepared in advance for them. Through his Spirit God will grant them continual supplies of grace so that they are able to bring forth the fruit of holiness in good works, to the glory of God. This grace "teaches us to say 'No' to ungodliness and worldly passions and to live self-controlled, upright and godly lives in this present age" (Titus 2:11,12).

A further argument against perseverance asserts that though there is a possibility of believers totally falling away, it is no greater than that of a sane man taking his own life. People will naturally avoid doing anything that could endanger their physical lives. In a similar way, it has been suggested, God has given to the saints the wisdom and prudence to keep from the sin which could destroy their souls. This ignores the forces of evil massed against the believer. One such enemy is indwelling sin (Romans 7:17,20). Paul calls this enemy "your old self, which is being corrupted by its deceitful desires" (Ephesians 4:22). All who have known anything of the strength of indwelling sin know that we need a greater power than common prudence to keep us from falling away eternally. We need the intercession of Christ. We "through faith are shielded by God's power until the coming of the salvation that is ready to be revealed" (I Peter 1:5).

Isaiah chapter four proves a source of great encouragment to God's people. Here, as in other scriptures, the glorious Branch of the Lord spoken of is the Lord Jesus Christ. Those to whom the promises are given are "those who are left in Zion" (verse 3). Who are they? They are the remnant according to the election of grace (Romans 11:5), whose names are in the Lamb's book of life from the creation of the world (Ephesians 1:4; Revelation 13:8). They have been rescued from the perishing mass of mankind, like a piece of wood snatched from a blaze that threatens to burn it up. Isaiah also describes them as the "daughter of Zion" – elect, redeemed and called of God. Justification, sanctification and perseverance are promised to them.

1. *Justification.* The Lord our righteousness covers them with the glorious robe of his own righteousness to hide their deformities and make them acceptable in his Father's sight.

2. *Sanctification.* Those who are called to be holy he makes holy by the work of Christ in them.

3. *Perseverance.* The pillar of cloud and of fire were a protection to the children of Israel in the wilderness. Isaiah refers to this when he says: "Upon all the glory shall be a defence (a covering)". The glory of Israel was the ark, a type of Christ. There are two parts to our spiritual glory. The first is outside of us. It is the love and favour of God toward us, by which he freely accepts us in Christ. The second is our sanctification, which is produced within us by the Spirit of holiness. He will never be completely dislodged from that believer's soul where he has once dwelt. The Holy Spirit will not allow the spirit of the world to take over his dwelling place. Believers' acceptance with God, their holiness from God, and his defence over them, freely given in Christ, make up the covenant of grace which cannot be broken.

12

We are not saying that believers can never sin. We are saying that they cannot sin away the Holy Spirit so as to become again children of the devil. This they were before they were born again (Ephesians 2:2,3).

God's relationship with his people is expressed by the prophet Jeremiah (31:33,34; 32:38-40). God promises to be their God. They will be his people.

1. *God accepts them freely.* "I will forgive their iniquity and I will remember their sin no more (Jeremiah 31:34).
2. *Both their sanctification and holiness must come from God.* "I will put my law in their inward parts, and write it in their hearts " (Jeremiah 31:33).
3. *The fear of God will never totally leave them.* "I will put my fear in their hearts, that they shall not depart from me" (Jeremiah 32:40). "I will give them one heart, and one way, that they may fear me for ever" (Jeremiah 32:39).

2.
God is unchangeable

God reveals the unchangeableness of his love towards his people by five ways in which he cannot change. They are:
1. his nature
2. his purposes
3. his covenant
4. his promises
5. his oath

The perseverance of the saints rests on each of these. We shall deal with these five ways in the next few chapters. In this chapter we consider God's own unchangeable nature.

In Malachi 3:6 God says: "I the Lord do not change". Then, as a consequence of this, he goes on to say: "So you, O descendants of Jacob, are not destroyed". Who are the descendants of Jacob that God speaks of? They are certainly not all the physical descendants of Jacob, but they are those who share his faith. As Paul says: "For they are not all Israel which are of Israel" (Romans 9:6). There were those who prided themselves on their descent from Abraham who were threatened by God with swift judgment because of their evil ways (Malachi 3:5). Christ was sent "to restore the tribes of Jacob and bring back those of

Israel I have kept" (Isaiah 49:6). Jacob's true sons are those who are born again "not of blood, nor of the will of the flesh, nor of the will of man, but of God" (John 1:13). God will never change his mind about his gift of effectual calling. Paul says in Romans 11:29: "God's gifts and his call are irrevocable".

Jacob's true descendants are those who possess the faith of Jacob. These are God's new elect Israel. God has entered into a new covenant with them in place of the earlier covenant which their forefathers broke (Jeremiah 31:31-34; Ezekiel 36:24-28; Hebrews 8:8-12). Those who enjoy the benefits of the new covenant do not deserve them. What was their spiritual state when God called them? It was one of death, darkness, ignorance and separation from God. There was nothing in them to cause God to show them his grace. Their sanctification and justification come from God alone.

One of the Lord's greatest consolations to his people is that they shall never be eternally separated from him. In Isaiah 40:27-31 Jacob and Israel declare their fear of being separated from God. How does God answer them? He asks them whether they have really understood the true nature of their God. He reminds them of his eternal nature, the greatness of his power, his unchangeableness and his infinite wisdom. This is what he will do for those who hope in the Lord. He will give them fresh strength; they will soar up as on eagles' wings; they will run without growing weary and they will walk and not faint. In answer to his people's fears, God says: "Jacob, my servant, don't be afraid. I have chosen you from eternity. You feel you are barren and unprofitable, parched and withered. I will change all that by giving you my Spirit. You will know that you belong to me and that I am your Lord and King, your

Redeemer from everlasting". When God assures us of his everlasting love for us on the grounds of his unchangeableness, it is not presumption to believe that he means what he says.

We should make a distinction between God's favour to a nation, such as the Jews, and his acts of saving grace to individuals. God dealt with his national people, the Jews, in outward blessings and punishments which distinguished them from the rest of the world. Their obedience to God as a nation affected his dealings with them. At times, therefore, he pulled down what he had built up. At other times he set up what he had earlier pulled down. Yet even these changes in his outward dealings with his national people still fulfilled his overall unchangeable purposes for them.

We may be sure that because God is unchangeable in his nature he will never forsake those whom he has freely accepted in Christ. Those so accepted can never become inpenitent apostates.

3.
God's purposes unchangeable

Let us now consider the unchangeableness of God's purposes which are another ground of assurance to the saints. These purposes are the eternal, infinitely wise and free acts of his will, quite independent of any cause outside himself.

In Isaiah 46:9-11 God declares that in contrast to all false gods he is the only God and that his purpose will stand. What he has purposed to do he will do. He knows beforehand the whole pattern of events from the beginning to the end. By his power he overrules the intentions of those he uses in such a way that they accomplish his will while freely doing their own. The unchangeable purposes of the Lord declare his eternal power and Godhead. Psalm 33:9-11 says: "He spoke, and it came to be; he commanded, and it stood firm . . . the plans of the Lord stand firm for ever, the purposes of his heart through all generations". By contrast, human beings constantly have to adapt their plans to changing circumstances, as in Proverbs 19:21: "Many are the plans in a man's heart, but it is the Lord's purpose that prevails". Since all things are present to God nothing can happen to take him by surprise. That almighty power which ensures that his purposes are carried out (Isaiah 14:24-27) is never arbitrary but always according to his infinite wisdom and holiness.

The doctrine of the perseverance of saints is declared in Romans 8:29 by the apostle Paul with great clarity and force. "We know that all things work together for good to them that love God, to them who are the called according to his purpose". What then is the "good" of those who love God, for which all things work so harmoniously together? It consists in their enjoyment of Christ and his love. God will so order all things that they will not fail to reach this highest enjoyment. In his wisdom and love he causes even the things that seem most to work against it to fulfil this end.

This comfort is given by God to those who are "called according to his purpose", who have responded to this effectual call by faith and obedience. They love God because their heart of stone has been taken away and they have been given a heart of flesh. In Romans 8:29-30 the calling of believers is preceded by their predestination and followed by their justification. God's intention in calling them is what the apostle elsewhere describes as the purposes of God according to election. His choosing of them by his grace is completely independent of any good in them which God could have foreseen and approved. God's approval of people is entirely because of his love and gracious acceptance of them in Christ and never the result of their loving God before being called. Still less is the believer's call the result of loving God. That is an impossibility. All faith and love in a believer are the fruit of God's effectual calling.

Notwithstanding the plain, unconditional statement of the promise of God given in Romans 8:28, attempts have been made to prove that it really is conditional upon believers keeping themselves from wickedness and unbelief. Of course it is true that this scripture gives no assurance that all things work together for the good of impenitent unbelievers. God's purpose is not that his believing people should be allowed to slip back into wickedness and unbelief but that they should be conformed to the image of his Son. It is God's will to safeguard his saints in their present experience of the love of Christ until they have the perfect enjoyment of its fulness in glory.

Jeremiah speaks of the eternal love of God to all the spiritual descendants of Jacob: "I have loved you with an everlasting love; I have drawn you with lovingkindness" (Jeremiah 31:3). These spiritual children are the remnant, elected by God's grace whom God foreknew (Romans 11:2,7). Paul writing to Timothy (II Timothy 2:19) comforts him (and with him all believers) by assuring him that "the foundation of God stands sure, having this seal, The Lord knows those who are his". This solid foundation is the good pleasure of the will of God which he purposed in himself to the praise of the glory of his grace. Paul's use of the word "foundation" emphasises the stability, strength and lasting qualities of God's will in supporting the whole fabric of the salvation of believers. On this unshakable foundation rest their preservation and perseverance. The apostasy of men like Hymenaeus and Philetus proved that they never had the faith of God's elect though they once seemed to be true believers. The purpose of God given here under the figure of a constructional foundation is said to be "sealed", as a legal document is sealed. That is to say, it is confirmed or established by the two-fold declaration: "The Lord knows those who are his", and "Everyone who confesses the name of the Lord must turn away from wickedness". These two statements cannot be separated.

Our Lord's purpose in coming down from heaven is clearly stated in John 6:37-40. He came to do his Father's will in every detail. Who are those for whom he came to do the Father's will? They are: "All that he has given me" (verse 39). Our Lord goes further in demonstrating the perfect harmony between himself and the Father when he says in his high priestly prayer: "They were yours; you gave them to me" (John 17:6). They are those who look to the Son and believe (John 6:40). What is the will of God for them? It is that none of them should be lost and that they might have eternal life and be raised up at the last day. In his prayer, the Lord mentions the everlasting life of believers before their being raised at the last day, so it is certain that the Father has committed the work of their preservation to the Son. Those who have been given to him shall never be lost.

Despite this assurance that Christ keeps and preserves his believing people, it has sometimes been argued from the apostasy of those who seemed at one time to run well, that true believers may yet fall from grace and be lost. Against such a view it may be asked: "At what point has the Keeper of Israel failed? Has he failed in faithfulness, in tenderness, or in power?" As a merciful and faithful High Priest he is well able to help those who are tempted (Hebrews 2:17,18). Or is it power he lacks? He said of himself: "All power is given unto me in heaven and in earth" (Matthew 28:18). "He is able to save completely those who come to God through him" (Hebrews 7:25).

Again it has been argued that though Christ will in no way cast out anyone coming to him, the one coming may yet turn back and never fully meet up with him.

In answer we may ask: "Is the one who is on his way to Christ, whom Christ is ready to receive, a believer or not? If he has no faith, how can he properly be said to be coming? If he has faith, how is it that he has not already come to Christ?"

It must be admitted that believers may be drawn aside into errors and false doctrines. Yet if they are, it is only for a while and never in a way that is inconsistent with their union with Christ their head, for his life is in them. Thus people may for a time be ignorant of certain fundamental doctrines of the faith, or even disbelieve them, and yet not be thought of as separated from Christ. We cannot accept that a true believer will persist in such denials since Christ promised that the Spirit will lead into all truth. There are, however, beliefs and ways of life that are inconsistent with the life of Christ in the soul. A complete renunciation of Christ would be such a case. Peter did deny his Lord when he was overcome by sudden temptation, though without any deliberate or premeditated intent. The Saviour however did not renounce Peter but prayed for him, and Peter repented and returned to following Christ. Therefore Peter's denials were not a complete renunciation of Christ.

In concluding this chapter, two other scriptures may be mentioned which speak expressly of the unchangeable purpose of God in the salvation of his people. The first is Ephesians 1:3-5: "Blessed be the God and Father of our Lord Jesus Christ who has blessed us ... chosen us ... and predestinated us unto the adoption of children by Jesus Christ unto himself, according to the good pleasure of his will". This eternal act of God is the fountain from which flows all the grace and favour of God in their justification, adoption and fruit-bearing through the

Spirit. God's aim in this act of his will is that we should be without blame before him in love (verse 4). The second scripture is II Thessalonians 2:13,14: "God has from the beginning chosen you to salvation through sanctification of the Spirit and belief of the truth . . . to the obtaining of the glory of our Lord Jesus Christ". Here again is revealed the same fountain of all spiritual and eternal mercy – God's choice of us by an everlasting act. What end does God have in view? Our salvation and the glory of our Lord Jesus Christ! He achieves his purpose in us by our calling, our sanctification and our justification by belief of the truth.

4.
God's covenant unchangeable

So far we have sought to show the unchangeable love that God has for his saints from a consideration of his own nature and purposes. We shall now see how the same truth is revealed in his covenant of grace. The basis of God's unchangeable favour towards his people lies, we may say, in his decrees and purposes. We learn about it from his covenant promise. Two texts of scripture serve to make this point.

The first text is God's promise to Abraham given in Genesis 17:7: "I will establish my covenant as an everlasting covenant between me and you and your descendants after you for the generations to come, to be your God and the God of your descendants after you". There was a limited fulfilment of this promise to Abraham in his natural descendants, the Jewish nation, but the true fulfilment of the covenant was in his spiritual descendants, the children of promise. These spiritual children would include people from many nations who would be blessed by God through Jesus Christ. All believers receive those blessings which faithful Abraham inherited because of this promise (Galatians 3:9). Ephesians 1:3 speaks of "every spiritual blessing". If perseverance in God's love is considered to be a spiritual blessing, as surely it must be, then not only Abraham but all faithful people throughout the world are blessed with it in Christ. David recognised that the "sure mercies" of which Isaiah and Paul spoke (Isaiah 55:3 and Acts 13:34) had as their origin the everlasting covenant God had made with him, ordered in all things and sure. To him this was all his salvation and all his desire (II Samuel 23:5).

The second scripture we refer to is Jeremiah 31:31-34. God assures Jeremiah that the new covenant he would make with the house of Israel was an everlasting covenant. It forever superseded the old covenant (Jeremiah 32:38-40). In this new covenant, God promised to write his law in their hearts and to remember their sin no more. He promised, too, that he would be their God and they should be his people. Sin separates God and man, in two ways. First, God must cast off the sinner because he is guilty. God's justice is such that strictly it requires him to do so. Second, sin itself through its power and deceitfulness causes people to go away from God until they are "filled with their own ways" (Proverbs 14:14). If, however, these causes of separation can be removed, God and man can be reconciled in peace and unity. This God had done. In Jeremiah 31:34 he promised: "I will forgive their iniquity and I will remember their sin no more." Through Christ the guilt of sin is removed in a way that brings the greatest honour to God's justice. God has set forth Christ to be a propitiation (or sacrifice of atonement) through faith in his blood; that is, he should be the one who would turn aside God's wrath by taking away sin (Romans 3:25). God declares that he will break the power and deceitfulness of sin in the believer's experience when he says: "I will put my law in their minds and write it on their hearts " (Jeremiah

31:33). And as if to add further emphasis, he says: "I will inspire them to fear me, so that they will never turn away from me" (Jeremiah 32:40).

Hebrews 8:9-12 contrasts the unchangeable covenant which was confirmed in the blood of Christ with the old covenant which depended on human fulfilment of its conditions. When two people enter into a covenant, or agreement, no-one can guarantee that it will be fulfilled if it depends on each of them. Both may fail to keep the agreement. But even if one remains true to what he has agreed, if the other breaks his promise the agreement is finished. So it was with God and Adam. God continued faithful but Adam proved faithless so that that covenant was made invalid. Similarly with a covenant between husband and wife. One party cannot guarantee that the whole covenant will be observed, as the other may prove faithless. God's new covenant is completely different. God has taken the sole responsibility for ensuring that it will not be broken. Praise God that he, having laid the foundation of his covenant in the blood of his dear Son, has not left it in our power to undo his great work of mercy.

God and man are separated at so great a distance by sin that they can only be brought together in some middle person, or mediator. This person is declared to be Christ Jesus himself (I Timothy 2:5) by whose blood the covenant is confirmed. He is the mediator of a better covenant established on better promises, who continues unchangeable because he is the same yesterday, today and for ever (Hebrews 13:8). All the promises of God are "yes" in Christ (II Corinthians 1:20). In his Son, God has ensured that all the promises of his covenant shall be fulfilled. By the death of his Son, God made his promises a legacy and bequeathed them to the people whom he had included in his covenant.

One of God's names that emphasises his faithfulness is, "The God who stands by his covenant". What has he promised to do in his covenant? First, that he will never forsake us. Second, that he will never allow us to forsake him. Based on such divine certainties, this covenant of grace can therefore never be subject to the unreliability and uncertainties of the wills of human beings in spite of those who have tried to argue to the contrary.

5.
God's general promises unchangeable

Let us now turn to the promises of God – the God who cannot lie – which assure us of his unchangeable love and favour to believers. It may be argued that certain of God's promises are conditional; that is, that they depend to some degree on the persons to whom they are made. Such promises might therefore not be fulfilled should there be any change in those to whom they have been given. We shall need to see later whether this is true of the particular promises we have in mind, but in the meantime let us look at the promises themselves. We shall call them "gospel promises" because of their nature and excellency. They are found, of course, not only in the New Testament but were given from the time that sin entered the world, for the encouragement of God's people under the old covenant.

In contrast to the gospel promises there were also promises given under the law, but in these "entering into life" was always linked with "keeping the commandments" (Matthew 19:17). Gospel promises are the free and gracious revelation of God's good will and love to sinners, through Christ, in the covenant of grace. We have already seen in chapter 4 how God promised to be their God in truth and faithfulness. He gave his Son for them, and to them, and he sent the Holy Spirit to abide with them. Each of the gospel promises shows the same love, the same Christ and the same Spirit. The promises are free and gracious because they are given only through the good will and pleasure of God. In the scriptures that which comes to us by promise is everywhere contrasted with what we have deserved or secured for ourselves (Galatians 3:18).

Jesus Christ is promised to us by God because of his love, free grace and mercy (John 3:16; Romans 5:8; I John 4:10). Some of the promises may seem to be conditional but because they are inseparably linked with God's promised gift of Christ they are, in reality, free and gracious. Gospel promises declare God's good will and love. Everything that speaks of grace and good will to sinners must be thought of as a promise of God. God's promises do not always refer only to the future. They may speak of things he has done in the past or is doing now. Note that it was to sinners that the promises were originally made. If the promises had not been for sinners, no-one could ever have benefited from them because the scripture declares that the whole world is held captive by sin (Galatians 3:22). All people are sin's prisoners until the promised salvation through faith in Jesus Christ sets them free. All deliverance from sin is by God's grace and all grace comes through his promise.

The revelation of God's good will to us is made through Christ. As II Corinthians 1:20 declares: "No matter how many promises God has made, they are 'Yes' in Christ". Christ is the guarantor, or surety, of the covenant, who has undertaken to do whatever is necessary both on God's part and ours to ensure that the covenant is carried out. We can therefore say that gospel promises are the expression of God's good will to us in a covenant of grace. Paul calls them "the covenants of the promise" (Ephesians 2:12). Strictly speaking the covenant and the promise (which is Christ) should be thought of in the singular but the apostle used the plural form because they have been given and renewed on several occasions. So Hebrews 8:6 speaks of the covenant of grace as being founded on better, or (as we might say) gospel, promises given by God who cannot lie (Titus 1:2).

What has God promised to do? In essence, he has promised that he will be our God, as he says to Jeremiah: "I will be their God and they will be my people" (Jeremiah 31:33). In order for him to be our God, two things are required:

1. that all which separates us from him must be removed and a perfect reconciliation made. This he does by giving Christ both to us and for us as our Saviour, our righteousness and our peace.

2. that we may be preserved for communion with him as our God and for the enjoyment of him as our reward. This he does by the gift of his Holy Spirit. Through the Spirit the Father has fitted us to share in the inheritance of the saints in the kingdom of light (Colossians 1:12). This promise of the Spirit occurs so frequently in both the Old and New Testaments that he is sometimes called "the promise of the covenant". In Acts 2:39, when Peter says "The promise is for you and your children" he is referring to the promise which Christ received from the Father called in verse 33 "the promised Holy Spirit".

From these two great promises, the gift of Christ and of the Holy Spirit, flow consolations of all kinds to believers. Here is everything they need to make them acceptable to God and to enjoy his presence. We can say, further, that anyone having an interest in any one of the promises has an interest in them all and in the love of God from which they flow. Even those promises of God which seem most conditional can be seen to spring from his unconditional love. God, who promises life to those who believe, has not set any condition on our part for his promised gift of faith, because we are all sinners. We may therefore make the following points about the nature of the promises of God:

1. *All God's promises are true and faithful; every one must be fulfilled.* His nature guarantees their accomplishment. Any failure would reflect on one or other of his unchangeable attributes. Even on the human level, no-one would make a solemn promise to do something when he knew that a change in circumstances might render him unable to fulfil his promise. How much more so is this the case when it is God who, knowing all things, gives his word of promise.

2. *We may be ignorant of many of the ways in which God has carried out his promises.* He may have fulfilled them to the letter even though we may be unaware of that fact.

3. *Even the conditional promises of God may be fulfilled in an absolute sense.* For example, in the statement, "He that believes shall be saved", an unbroken connection is declared between faith and salvation. The statement is true whether anyone, in fact, believes or not. Conditional promises may simply declare the will of God as, for example, "He that keeps the commandments shall live", or they may show that the things spoken in them are the means by which God's will is to be brought about.

4. As has been shown before, the promises which have to do with the saints' perseverance are of two kinds. Either they show how God's favour is continually toward them (that is, their justification), or they have to do with their continued obedience to God (that is, their sanctification).

Even those promises concerning our sanctification which appear to be conditional are really absolute. God has promised believers that they will remain under his covenant for ever. Some people have argued: "Yes, but this is on the condition that they do not willingly cast off Christ's yoke or allow themselves to be led astray". We may answer: "Is this not really saying that provided they stay with him, they will stay with him?" – which is no argument at all! God draws us with kindness to follow and stay with him because he loves us with an everlasting love.

An important purpose of God in giving the promises is to comfort believers whatever condition they may be in. As God said to Joshua: "I will be with you; I will never leave you or forsake you" (Joshua 1:5). Some people argue that God makes his promises not to individuals but to the qualifications those individuals possess. We reply that the promises must certainly be kept but if their fulfilment depends on these qualifications then they are made to conditions, not to persons. God says otherwise. He has expressly called his elect people "the children of promise" (Romans 9:8). We see then that the things that are promised are often dependent on each other, yet the promises themselves are absolute.

The fact that God's promises will certainly be fulfilled does not rule out the use of suitable means. When God promised Paul in Acts 27 that there would be no loss of any man's life in the ship's company, it was not inconsistent with the promise for Paul to say "unless these men stay with the ship you cannot be saved".

Saints can, then, rest wholly on the faithfulness of God to his promises. As Paul says in I Thessalonians 5:24: "The one who calls you is faithful and he will do it".

6.
God's particular promises illustrated

Continuing our consideration of the promises of God, we now move on from general to particular promises. The Lord gave a very personal promise to Joshua as he was poised to cross the river Jordan: "I will be with you; I will never leave you or forsake you" (Joshua 1:5). At first sight this may seem to be intended only for Joshua, yet the saints of God have learned to use it for themselves as the Holy Spirit has applied it to their own circumstances. Certainly, as the Israelite army general chosen by God for the conquest of Canaan, Joshua needed the promise for his own encouragement. Nevertheless, this promise is one of many which are recorded in the Old Testament for our consolation also. We too have learned that "everything that was written in the past was written to teach us, so that through endurance and the encouragement of the scriptures we might have hope" (Romans 15:4). Believers today may say with no less confidence than the psalmist: "The Lord is my helper" (Psalm 118:6,7; Hebrews 13:6). Thus the promise originally given to Joshua becomes an inducement to obedience by the godly of every generation and a testimony to the good will of the Lord to his saints.

God promises in Psalm 89:30-34 not to take his

lovingkindness away from his people nor in faithfulness to break his covenant with them even if they fail to keep his commandments. Should they do so, he will correct them with chastening either in the outward circumstances of their lives or inwardly by withdrawing the felt sense of his presence. God will not cast them off, though they deserve it because of their sin. God has pledged his lovingkindness, his faithfulness, his covenant, his promise and his oath. Nor is it a purely negative action on his part that he will not forsake them. He gives a positive assurance that he will continue his presence with them. As he promised in Isaiah 27:3 he will carefully tend his vineyard. Barren though it may seem to be for a time, yet by continual watering he will make it a vineyard producing the best red wine. The reason he does this is not for anything in them but for his great Name's sake. The "Name" of God stands for everything by which he is made known to us – all his attributes, his will and his glory. When God does anything for his great Name's sake, he reveals his nature and displays his glory. We see his perfect faithfulness and grace in Jesus Christ. All his goodness and kindness come from his nature "who works out everything in conformity with the purpose of his will" (Ephesians 1:11). The assurance that God's goodness and mercy would follow him all his days caused David to declare so confidently: "I will dwell in the house of the Lord for ever" (Psalm 23:6). David's response to God's promises was a promise on his part to constant obedience.

Psalm 125:2 is a powerful testimony to God's everlasting presence with his people. "As the mountains surround Jerusalem, so the Lord surrounds his people both now and for ever more". Just as it is impossible for a man to overturn the foundations of the

36

mountains that surround Jerusalem, so it is impossible for the enemies of God's people to prevail over them to their eternal destruction. By these enemies he means not only human adversaries but their greater, spiritual foes.

Lest any should doubt his gracious intention God confirms it in Isaiah 54:7-10 with an unbreakable oath: " 'I swore that the waters of Noah would never again cover the earth. So now I have sworn . . . that my unfailing love for you will not be shaken, nor my covenant of peace be removed', says the Lord, who has compassion on you" (verses 9 and 10). In spite of the sinfulness of mankind since the flood God has remained faithful to his covenant. The world has not been destroyed a second time by a universal flood, nor will it ever be.

There have been those who would pervert the promises into an encouragement to sin. Such have no sense of the obligation of love on those who have been saved from sin's condemnation. They know nothing of the love of the Father, the blood of the Son and the grace of the Holy Spirit. But through these very great and precious promises we escape the corruption in the world caused by evil desires. By such promises we even share in the divine nature (II Peter 1:3,4). It follows, therefore, as Paul says in II Corinthians 7:1: "Since we have these promises . . . let us purify ourselves from everything that contaminates body and spirit and let us strive for perfection out of reverence for God. God forbid that we should go on sinning, so that grace may increase" (Romans 6:1,2).

In Hosea 2:19,20 God uses the most intimate of human relationships, that of husband and wife, to declare the closeness of his relationship with his people. "I will betroth you to me for ever; I will

37

betroth you in righteousness and justice, in love and compassion. I will betroth you in faithfulness, and you will acknowledge the Lord". The previous verses give the background to this remarkable declaration – the threat of the Lord's judgments against the entire idolatrous nation of Israel. Then in verse 14, in a sudden change of attitude, God pledges himself to give to the true Israelites among them four great blessings. They will be converted by the gospel, delivered from idolatry, protected from everything that would spoil their quietness and peace and be betrothed to him in an everlasting covenant of grace. It is clear that these promises go beyond temporal blessings to include all the spiritual blessings of the gospel.

Who are they to whom such promises are given? They are God's children according to God's promise. They are those whom God separates from unbelievers and to whom he speaks words of comfort. Just as the Israelites were brought out of Egypt into the wilderness, so God separates his people from the lusts of sin and leads them to delight themselves in him. In the wilderness the Israelites did not know what to do or where to go but were wholly dependent on God to go before and lead them. This was a time of love when the Lord drew them away from their false ideas with his tender words. God speaks to them again in Isaiah 40:1,2: " 'Comfort, comfort my people', says your God". Likewise, believers nowadays long for their iniquities to be pardoned.

God promises to unite believers to himself for ever. He does this in the full knowledge of what they once were and would still be apart from him. He knows them intimately but promises that they too shall know the Lord. He does more than woo them; he says: "I will betroth you".

John 10:27-29 speaks to us of the Saviour's knowledge of his sheep which ensures their eternal safety. The omnipotence of God makes sure that they remain his sheep and that no-one will ever pluck them out of his hand. The perseverance of all the sheep is secured by the Saviour's words: "I give unto my sheep eternal life and they shall never perish . . . no-one can snatch them out of my Father's hand".

7.
Christ's work on earth

We shall now turn to the mediation of Christ. He is the
guarantor (or surety) of the Father's faithfulness to us
and the surety for us of our faithfulness to him. We ask
then: "What have Christ's sacrifice and intercession to
do with the perseverance of the saints?". There is no
doubting the fact of his intercession. "He is able to
save completely (for ever) those who come to God
through him, because he always lives to intercede for
them" (Hebrews 7:25). The sacrifice of Christ also
safeguards the salvation of his saints. It does this in
two ways:

1. *It removes everything that separates believers from God.*
This may be summed up as (a) the guilt of sin and (b)
the power of sin and Satan. The guilt of sin is removed
because Christ has obtained eternal redemption for us
(Hebrews 9:12). Through his death we have
forgiveness of sins for ever (Ephesians 1:7). The Old
Testament animal sacrifices were a pattern of Christ's
death. They were offered year by year on the altar but
they could never make perfect those who came to God
with them, or acquit the worshippers of sin. If sin had
been taken away by the sacrifices offered as the law
required, the worshippers would not have needed to

come time after time to repeat the same sacrifices (Hebrews 10:1-3). By contrast, Christ's offering of himself once for all as a sacrifice for sin makes perfect for ever those who are set apart to God. Those for whom Christ died are no longer under the condemnation of God for their sin. Christ reconciles the Father to us, making him "at one" towards us, and brings in for us an everlasting righteousness which God will accept. The question asked in Romans 8:34 – "Who is he that condemns?" – is fully answered: "Christ Jesus died – more than that, was raised to life".

Notwithstanding the death of Christ, many live painfully aware of the guilt of sin all their lives. Yet its guilt is completely taken away from all those for whom Christ died so that it will never separate them eternally from God. In the obedience and death of his Son God made a way by which his eternal purposes of saving grace could be revealed.

The declared judgment of God is that those who commit sin deserve to die (Romans 1:32). Yet by his righteousness Christ has provided a way by which God may justly receive his sinning creatures to favour again. God's justice is satisfied not by anything we have done but by what Christ has done. In Christ's sacrifice the law of God is fulfilled. This law of God is a reflection of his own holinss. It calls for a curse on all who fail to do everything written in it. Christ by his death put himself under the curse of the law for those for whom he died. Written into God's law is this great curse on all who break the law. But in the law there is only one curse; it has not another for those on whose behalf Christ died. "Christ redeemed us from the curse of the law by becoming a curse for us" (Galatians 3:13). "God made him who had no sin to be sin for us, so that in him we might become the righteousness of

God" (II Corinthians 5:21). God's truth is satisfied by the sacrifice of Christ. At the beginning God declared a warning against sin. "You must not eat from the tree of the knowledge of good and evil, for when you eat of it you will surely die" (Genesis 2:17). The sacrifices of old seemed to provide an answer in that there was a death – that of a victim. But the life of an animal could never be thought of as reaching a level of worth that God's judgment on sin requires. Hebrews 10:4 makes this plain: "It is impossible for the blood of bulls and goats to take away sins". What is Christ's answer to this? "Here I am . . . I have come to do your will, O God". Will he be acceptable to the Father? Yes, he certainly will, because of his intrinsic worth.

God's justice is upheld by the sacrifice of Christ. Because of it God fulfils every part of the covenant made with Christ on behalf of those for whom he is the mediator. Some have raised the question: "What if any of those for whom Christ died should themselves die without being born again? Would they not be overtaken by the justice and condemning power of the law of God in spite of Christ's death?" Put this way, it is impossible to ask this question because Christ died so that those for whom he died should be born again and live. This they will be, in due time; none of them will die in their sins.

Some might argue that if Christ has so satisfied God's justice and fulfilled the law on behalf of all for whom he died, there is no need for them to believe. Or, if they do believe, there is no need for them to live a holy life. This argument is completely false. Though the justice, law and truth of God are satisfied with regard to their sins, God still requires his people to live by the law of faith. Faith gives God all the glory for his grace, exalts Jesus Christ, and empties the sinner of any trust in himself for salvation. We cannot think of the freedom from condemnation that the death of Christ brings without also remembering that Christ purchased for us the gift of the Holy Spirit and his grace. By the working of his grace in our hearts we are not only set free from the guilt of sin but from its power also. We who are born again have died to sin that it should not reign in us. Those who think that faith, holiness and communion with God are only means for escaping the wrath to come have little understanding of what it means to be changed into the image of the glory of God. These graces make us fruitful in God's service here and prepare us to be made in his likeness hereafter.

By his death Christ obtained eternal redemption for us, which is the forgiveness of sins (Hebrews 9:12; Ephesians 1:7). Forgiveness of sins applied to the consciences of believers requires the activity of faith so that Christ may be received according to the promise: "Who has become for us wisdom from God – that is, our righteousness, holiness and redemption" (I Corinthians 1:30). Christ himself bore our sins in his body on the tree and the Father accepted his discharge of our debt. Yet this freedom from condemnation does not set believers free from the necessity of obeying God.

Our union with Christ is such that those things which he has done for us, we are said to do together with him. Thus, we die with him and are raised again with him. With him also we enter into the holy place. With all this being done for us by our Head, can death now have any authority over us? As the apostle argues in II Corinthians 5:14,15: "We are convinced that one died for all and therefore all died (that is all those for whom he died)". They died in him when he, as their representative, died and took upon himself the curse due to their sins so that they in future might live to him who died for them.

The agreement between the Father and the Son required that the Saviour should make his soul an offering for sin. By this, he would do what the sacrifices of bulls and goats stood for but could never actually perform. The Father dealt with his Son in perfect justice, not reducing the punishment that Christ took upon himself. Now that the ransom has been paid, shall not the prisoner be set free? With the debt paid, the law has no power against the original debtor.

Our fallen nature does not allow us to do any good thing towards God. If we are to be quickened into newness of life and have faith towards Jesus Christ, it must be by the work of the Holy Spirit in us. By the Spirit God works in us so that we both want and want to do what pleases him (Philippians 2:13). We are blessed with every spiritual blessing in Christ (Ephesians 1:3). In a special way this means the Holy Spirit himself. He gives us the faith to receive the atonement, or the reconciliation, with which God is completely satisfied.

We see therefore that everything to do with our salvation is brought about by the mediation of Christ. Christ's mediation springs from the glorious purpose of God in salvation and effectively brings it about. This act of the will of God is known in the scriptures as "election" or "predestination" or "the purpose of his will in Christ Jesus". Of itself it is not strictly speaking the act of forgiveness nor are those so chosen justified in any sense by it. It is through the mediation of the blood of Christ that we are reconciled to God. God absolves those for whom Christ died from the sentence and curse of the law of God. By sending the Spirit of his Son into their hearts, he leads them on into obedience and sanctification.

The Saviour ensures the love of the saints to God by taking away everything that might cause them to depart from God. What is it that makes believers turn away from God? The answer to that question may be summed up as Satan and his works. Satan is called the god of this world. The world under Satan's control is under God's curse. Satan uses the world as an instrument to hurt us and tempt us to go away from God. The world has no power of itself to do this, but only as Satan uses it. Jesus encouraged his disciples: "Take heart! I have overcome the world" (John 16:33). How does Christ deal with Satan? On the cross he conquered and broke Satan's power, binding the strong man and spoiling his goods.

There are two ways by which the blood of Christ breaks the power of Satan over God's elect:

a. He takes away the right which Satan had by sin to rule over God's elect. Satan rules over unbelievers with the terror of death and hell. He keeps innumerable souls in cruel bondage. Some he even drives to commit barbarous cruelties in an endeavour to make their own atonement for their sins.

b. Satan not only rules over men, he rules in them, because he rules in the children of disobedience (Ephesians 2:2). How then does Christ break the dominion of Satan over God's elect? In the first place by his own death which strips Satan of his power over them. All Satan's power lies in death. Death came into the world through sin. Jesus Christ, by taking away sin through his death on the cross, destroyed the whole authority of Satan. And in the second place Christ takes away the ability of Satan to exercise his power. He binds the strong man and leads him captive. Christ destroys Satan and his works. "The reason the Son of God appeared was to destroy the devil's work" (I John 3:8). He not only binds the strong man armed, he spoils his goods. By Christ's death, the believer's old self is crucified so that the body of sin might be rendered powerless (Romans 6:6).

Summing up this section we may say that the death of Christ so takes away the guilt of sin that it will never be able to turn the love of God away from believers. Christ so breaks the rule of Satan and the power of sin that they will never be able wholly to turn away from God.

2. *The Holy Spirit comes to God's elect through the mediation of Christ because of the new covenant.* Spiritual graces, like the gift of faith, do not come to us as the result of God's providential dealings with men. Faith to receive the pardon of sin does not spring from a covenant of works. The mercies of the covenant are obtained from the mediator of the new covenant, who is Christ. As Hebrews 9:15 says: "For this reason Christ is the mediator of a new covenant, that those who are called may receive the promised eternal inheritance – now that he has died as a ransom to set them free from the sins committed under the first covenant". That promised inheritance was in a special way the Holy Spirit who was sent from the Father as the answer to Christ's intercession (John 14:16,17). Christ encourages us to ask for the Holy Spirit from the Father so that we might have a fuller revelation of Christ to us (John 16:14).

Some people may fear that, although they readily admit that the Holy Spirit is given to believers, they might foolishly and finally reject him and he would not return. Should they do so, would it not increase their condemnation more than if they had not received him at all? (Romans 8:14,15) The promises of God – Father, Son and Holy Spirit – show the facts to be otherwise:

a. There is the Father's promise in Isaiah 59:21: "'As for me, this is my covenant with them', says the Lord. 'My Spirit who is on you, and my words that I have put in your mouth will not depart from your mouth . . . from this time on and for ever', says the Lord."

b. There is the Son's witness to the permanent presence of his Spirit with those who believe. In John 14:16 he says: "I will ask the Father, and he will give you another Counsellor to be with you for ever – the Spirit of truth". This assurance applies not only to the disciples to whom he spoke but to all believers throughout succeeding generations (John 17:20).

c. Finally we have the Spirit's witness. As the Father and Son gave their testimony in a word of promise, so the Spirit bears his own distinct testimony as he performs his work. II Corinthians 1:22 speaks of God setting his seal of ownership on us and putting his Spirit in our hearts as a deposit, guaranteeing what is to come. Sealing is a legal term derived from common practice in civil transactions. A seal is affixed, and duly witnessed, for two reasons:

i. to ensure secrecy and security to the things sealed;

ii. to make sure that what has to be done is done. In the first sense, coins or other articles are sealed up in bags and kept securely, no-one daring to break the seals. In the second sense, legal documents of all kinds are made valid by the seals affixed to them. So the sealing of the Spirit is, in this second sense, the means by which the promises are confirmed to the believer.

Sealing in the first sense is also involved when believers are said to be sealed for the day of redemption (Ephesians 4:30). Their safety and preservation are assured by the Spirit to the full enjoyment of what Christ has purchased for them.

8.
The Spirit lives in believers

We shall next consider how the Holy Spirit lives with those to whom he is given. Although at first sight this may not appear to be directly related to the question of the perseverance of the saints, yet because it affects their life of faith and walk with God it has an important bearing on it. One of the great promises of the covenant of grace is that the Spirit should dwell in us. In Ezekiel 36:27 God declares: "I will put my Spirit in you and move you to follow my decrees and be careful to keep my laws". God had already promised his people in the preceding verse: "I will give you a new heart and put a new spirit in you". Though this can be taken to mean a renewal of the attitude of their own spirits towards God, yet it must primarily mean the promised indwelling of his renewing Spirit because it is by him that our spirits are graciously restored. This indwelling of his Spirit comes to us as one of the Lord's great covenant blessings, as he says in Isaiah 59:21: " 'This is my covenant with them' says the Lord. 'My Spirit who is on you, and my words that I have put in your mouth will not depart from your mouth . . . from this time on and for ever', says the Lord". This promise of the Spirit is further echoed in the words of Jesus to his disciples: "How much more will your Father in heaven give the Holy Spirit to those who ask him" (Luke 11:13).

David, conscience-stricken because of his sin and feeling that all the graces of the Spirit were almost dead within him, cried out in Psalm 51:11: "Do not cast me from your presence or take your Holy Spirit from me". He acknowledged that his greatest need was sanctification, which he longed to be renewed in him by the Holy Spirit. Paul emphasises that the test of the spirituality of believers is their indwelling by the Spirit. "If anyone does not have the Spirit of Christ, he does not belong to Christ" (Romans 8:9). Paul is speaking not just of a spiritual grace but of the Holy Spirit himself – "the Spirit of him who raised Jesus from the dead" (verse 11). In verse 15 the Holy Spirit is called "the Spirit of sonship". Through him we recognise God as our Father. Paul assures believers that they who have been adopted as children into God's family have the privilege of calling him their Father. "Because you are sons, God sent the Spirit of his Son into our hearts, the Spirit who calls out 'Abba, Father'" (Galatians 4:6).

Some may argue that though the Spirit may be said to dwell in us, it is only in the graces he gives, not himself personally. The scriptures make a distinction between the Spirit and his graces. This is well illustrated in Romans 5:5: "God has poured out his love into our hearts by the Holy Spirit, whom he has given us". Here the love of God, either as a sense of his love to us or of our love to him, must clearly be thought of as a special grace given to us. But this grace must not be confused with the Holy Spirit by whom it is poured into our hearts.

In the scriptures, the Holy Spirit is shown to be a person and not an impersonal grace. The personality

of the Spirit is emphasised in three ways:
1. his personal titles
2. his personal acts
3. those situations in which he is personally found
Let us consider these three ways.

1. His personal titles. The apostle John says of the indwelling Spirit: "The one who is in you is greater than the one who is in the world" (I John 4:4). Our Lord, speaking to the disciples of the Comforter (or Counsellor), the Spirit of truth, says that he was to stay with them for ever. They would know him, "for he lives with you and will be in you" (John 14:16,17).

2. His personal acts. Romans 8:11 speaks specifically of the work of the Holy Spirit: "If the Spirit of him who raised Jesus from the dead is living in you, he who raised Christ from the dead will also give life to your mortal bodies through his Spirit who lives in you". And Romans 8:16: "The Spirit himself testifies with our spirit that we are God's children".

3. Situations in which he is personally found. In I Corinthians 3:16 the saints are described as a temple in which God dwells: "Don't you know that you yourselves are God's temple and that God's Spirit lives in you?" A further reference to the Holy Spirit living in believers is in I Corinthians 6:19 where the apostle Paul used that fact as a powerful prohibition against sexual sins by believers: "Do you not know that your body is a temple of the Holy Spirit, who is in you, whom you have received from God?" In Paul's day, a pagan temple was evil because of the evil god associated with it. But believers are the temple of the living God because the Spirit willingly lives in them.

53

Clearly, impersonal graces cannot be said to dwell in a temple. They are qualitites given to those who have them.

There are important effects in the lives of those in whom the Spirit dwells, and benefits too. The first is a spiritual union with the Lord Jesus Christ. The result of this work of the Spirit in our experience is communion with Christ. The same Spirit who dwells in him also dwells in us so that, as Peter says, we are made to share in the divine nature (II Peter 1:4). Christ said that this union arises from the eating of his flesh and the drinking of his blood (John 6:56). Many people were offended by those words because they could not understand what he was saying. Jesus had to tell them: "The Spirit gives life; the flesh counts for nothing" (John 6:63). By the indwelling of the life-giving Spirit we share the life of Christ. In his high priestly prayer in John 17 Christ asked that his people might know this union with himself (verse 21). The unity of believers with each other, for which he also prayed and which makes them as one body, comes from Christ as their Head. The Saviour said that this union is a reflection of his own union with the Father: "I in them and you in me" (John 17:23).

The scriptures give many illustrations of the union between Christ and his people. A common one is that of head and members together making one body. Christ is the head of the body, the church (Colossians 1:18), of which he is also the Saviour (Ephesian 5:23). By knowledge of the Son of God and with increasing maturity, believers will in all things grow up into him who is the head, that is, Christ (Ephesians 4:13,15). "From him the whole body . . . grows and builds itself up in love, as each part does its work" (verse 16). They become one indivisible body through the work of the life-giving Spirit living in them.

One of the commonest of the illustrations in the scriptures for the relationship between Christ and his people is that of husband and wife. Quoting Genesis 2:24 Paul sees this relationship typifying at the very dawn of history what would happen in the future. "For this reason a man will leave his father and mother and be united to his wife, and the two will become one flesh. This is a profound mystery – but I am talking about Christ and the church" (Ephesians 5:31,31).

Another illustration is that of a tree – vine or olive. Christ said: "I am the vine; you are the branches" (John 15:5). "Remain in me and I will remain in you" (verse 4). And with the olive tree, those branches which are grafted in are nourished by the same sap that is elsewhere in the root and other branches, so that they bear fruit. The same fruit-bearing Spirit is in Christ and in his people. This Spirit was in Christ the Son of God without limit (John 3:34) and is communicated to us from Christ.

The indwelling Spirit gives a completely new life to us who were dead in trespasses and sins. Christ is also said to be our life, as the apostle claims in Colossians 3:4. Christ lives in me, he tells us, in Galatians 2:20. We see then that the expressions "Christ dwells in you" and "His Spirit dwells in you" mean the same thing.

The indwelling Spirit gives direction and guidance to those in whom he dwells so that they may know how they ought to live. Paul in Romans 8:14 speaks of the leading of the Spirit which only the children of God have. "Those who are led by the Spirit of God are sons of God". The Spirit leads in two ways: (a) He shows the children of God what the way is and (b) supports them in it. In other words, the word of God gives us God's rule for our lives and the Spirit effectually strengthens us to walk in the pathway God has marked out for us. The Spirit helps our spiritual understanding to grow so that we know what the will of the Lord for us is. Our understanding of the gospel does not come to us as the result of our natural abilities but by the revelation of God through the Spirit. The word of God clearly points the way in which we should go and, as every believer can say, is a "lamp to my feet and a light for my path" (Psalm 119:105). A light may shine brightly on the pathway of a blind man but it will not help him unless his sight is restored. Similarly, unless the Spirit of light shines in our hearts and minds, we are "blind, or shortsighted" (II Peter 1:9).

It is possible to have a natural understanding of the truth and yet for the "light in us to be darkness" (Matthew 6:23). We may recognise, and even appreciate, the truth of God's word and yet it is ineffective in our lives if it is not received with faith (Hebrews 4:2). "The man without the Spirit does not accept the things that come from the Spirit of God . . . because they are spiritually discerned" (I Corinthians 2:14). But when the Holy Spirit comes to sinners, he guides them into all truth (John 16:13). As John says, the anointing they receive from him remains in them and they do not need anyone to teach them (I John 2:27).

As was said previously, the Spirit guides believers by graciously giving them light and power. He makes truth shine gloriously and it becomes attractive to the believer, who receives it gladly. God's Spirit poured out on us is like streams in the desert (Isaiah 35:5,6). Strength is given as well as light. The blind see, the ears of the deaf are unstopped, the lame leap like a deer and the dumb shout for joy. The Spirit not only shows spiritual truths in a general way, he also explains individual truths. These also are gladly received by the believer.

Many people do not have the Spirit of Christ living in them. Romans 1:21,22 says that "their thinking became futile and their foolish hearts were darkened. Although they claimed to be wise, they became fools". Other people make some progress in spiritual understanding but know nothing of the power of truth in their lives. They look at spiritual matters only in a natural way.

The indwelling Spirit supports believers in their burdens and trials. He comforts troubled believers in two ways. The first way is the one Christ used to strengthen his disciples. The Comforter reminds us of what Christ taught (John 14:26). The second way is that the Spirit strengthens our spiritual life and revives our spirits. Paul found God's grace in him was such that he could even glory in his sufferings (Romans 5:3). So not only does God's grace make us patient in suffering because it gives us strength to bear it, but we can even rejoice. That same verse tells us that "suffering produces perseverance; perseverance, character; and character, hope". And this all happens because "God has poured out his love into our hearts by the Holy Spirit whom he has given us" (verse 5).

One of the graces the Spirit gives is restraint. In this way he keeps within bounds the strong but improper desires of human beings, even of those who do not know him. And for believers, God promises to put his law in their minds and to write it on their hearts (Jeremiah 31:33). He makes them ready to do his whole will gladly. When believers are strongly tempted by Satan, the Spirit restrains them from doing evil.

Peter denied his Lord with curses but was then restrained by Christ's look so that he was overcome by repentance and grief. He went outside and wept bitterly (Matthew 26:75). Believers often feel God's restraint on them, subduing the natural inclinations of their hearts.

The Spirit daily renews our spiritual life by his sanctifying grace without which our souls would wither. The Spirit is like the sap which flows in the olive tree, keeping the branches fruitful and flourishing. He constantly fills our lamps with fresh oil and puts new vigour into our spirits (Psalm 92:10). David rejoiced that God was for ever satisfying his mouth with good things (Psalm 103:5). What are these good things? They are surely the same as the Saviour taught his disciples to ask for from the Father. "If you, then, though you are evil, know how to give good gifts to your children, how much more will your Father which is in heaven give good gifts to those who ask him?" (Matthew 7:11). From the parallel passage in Luke 11:13, it is clear he is referring to the gift of the Holy Spirit. All spiritual graces are the fruit of the Spirit (Galatians 5:22,23). In a tree, if the root is not always producing fresh sap the fruit will quickly wither. So Paul prays for the saints in Ephesus that they "being rooted and established in love . . . may be filled to the measure of all the fullness of God" (Ephesians 3:17,19).

The Spirit is like a never-failing fountain continually pouring out living waters of grace. As Christ said to the woman of Samaria: "Whoever drinks the water I give him will never thirst. Indeed, the water I give him will become in him a spring of water welling up to eternal life" (John 4:14). The water promised to that woman was the Holy Spirit. "Whoever believes in me, as the scripture has said, streams of living water will flow from within him. By this he meant the Spirit, whom those who believed in him were later to receive" (John 7:38,39). The person who has this Spirit of grace, this fountain of living water, will never know spiritual, eternal, thirst.

There are two kinds of thirst. There is a natural physical thirst which returns even after it is satisfied. Its parallel is the spiritual thirst God ascribes to wicked people in Isaiah 65:13. Their hunger and thirst are due to a total lack of God's grace. There is also a thirst after good things: "Blessed are those who hunger and thirst for righteousness for they will be filled" (Matthew 5:6). Peter encourages God's elect, who are strangers in the world, to develop this kind of thirst: "Like newborn babies, crave pure spiritual milk, so that by it you may grow up in your salvation, now that you have tasted that the Lord is good" (I Peter 2:2,3). The Spirit originates and encourages this kind of thirst.

So we can sum up Christ's promise in this way. Those to whom the Spirit is given to live with them for ever will never be reduced to total want; they will certainly persevere.

9.
Christ prays for believers

Many have already written about Christ's intercession and demonstrated how it completes the perfect salvation of believers. They have shown that the high priest in Old Testament times, who entered the holy of holies each year with blood on behalf of the people, vividly illustrates Christ's heavenly intercession (Hebrews 9:7). It is proposed, therefore, not to repeat this but to consider only how Christ intercedes for believers in order that they may be preserved in the love and power of the Father.

Christ has appeared for us in the presence of God (Hebrews 9:24) to plead as the advocate for our defence before God's judgment seat. The scriptures say that "he is able to save completely those who come to God through him, because he always lives to intercede for them" (Hebrews 7:25). What does he ask for those for whom he pleads? Is it that they, already being and continuing as believers, may be saved? Or is it that they may believe and continue as believers and be saved?

Let us examine the first of these alternatives. Christ does not need to pray for this, because it is an established principle of the gospel that "he that believes shall be saved". The truth and unchangeableness of God ensure that it will be so. This declaration of God cannot fail even though not a single person should continue believing to the end. If Christ only intercedes for this, the salvation of the church is not guaranteed. Surely the purpose of Christ's intercession must go beyond this uncertainty.

Let us look more closely at what the entrance of the high priest into the holy of holies on the Day of Atonement means. It is a representation of Christ's intercession. Before the high priest entered, a sacrifice had already been offered on the altar and the blood shed that was to be taken into the holy place. The entering in of the high priest was in order to complete the work of atonement and make peace with God on behalf of those for whom the sacrifice was made. The priest entering with the blood was to offer it for himself and for the errors of the people (Hebrews 9:7) but the offering was a continuation of the act of sacrifice already made on the altar outside in the temple court. The entering of the high priest represented the taking away of the guilt of the sins of the people and their continued peace with God. In a parallel but surer way Christ's intercession ensures the deliverance of believers from the guilt of sin and preserves them in the love and favour of God.

Christ's high-priestly prayer in John 17 may be thought of as the incense with which he entered the holy place. He entered heaven with this sweet perfume, sprinkled with his own blood. Thus he prays on behalf of those who truly believe in him: "Holy Father, protect them by the power of your name – the name you gave me – so that they may be one as we are one" (John 17:11). On the eve of his death he prays for them that they may be kept from sin and everything that would hinder their union with himself. If those for whom Christ prays are not kept in the love of God, either Christ's plea for them remains unanswered or the Father is powerless to keep them. Such is the strength of their own inward corruptions and of temptation from without that, left to themselves, they would never to able to hold out to the end. That is why Christ makes such a powerful plea to the Father for them. He pleads: "Keep them through your name – let your grace prove sufficient for them". The Lord Jesus recognises that the world in which his believing people live is deceitful and set in opposition against them. He does not pray, however, that they should be taken out of the world but that they may be kept and preserved from the power of evil. He has in mind not only his apostles around him but all who would believe on him to the end of the world (verse 20). We can see then that in his intercession Christ asks for the safe-keeping of believers in the love and power of God. His prayer is that they may be preserved in their communion with God against everything that would seek to break it. To say that believers can only be preserved if they do not wilfully depart from God is to say that they will be preserved only if they preserve themselves.

In Romans 8 we see how good an argument Paul uses to establish the certainty of the perseverance of believers. In verses 33 and 34 he says: "Who will bring any charge against those whom God has chosen? It is God who justifies. Who is he that condemns? Christ Jesus, who died – more than that, who was raised to life – is at the right hand of God and is also interceding for us". The freedom from condemnation of justified believers is based on the sacrifice and intercession of Christ. Who shall condemn? It is Christ that died. Believers are free from condemnation because all their sins were laid on Christ and punished in him. By his death he perfectly satisfied the justice of God for them. God cannot, therefore, punish them for anything. Not only has Christ died but he is risen, is at the right hand of God and makes intercession for them. The resurrection of Christ means that he is acquitted of all the sins that were put on him (and we in him). "After he had provided purification for sins, he sat down at the right hand of the Majesty in heaven" (Hebrews 1:3). This is the fullest declaration possible of the Father's acceptance of the work he had promised to do. Having now almighty power as the risen and glorified Lord, he shows his good will and care for our salvation by interceding for us. We can say then that those against whom no charge can be brought cannot in any way be separated from the love of God in Christ. They can never totally and finally abandon faith and fall out of God's favour.

10.
How the doctrine of final perseverance is to be used

What the scriptures say about the perseverance of the saints cannot fail to have a bearing on their obedience and their comfort. Their obedience, of course, matters more than their comfort because it gives greater honour to God. The obedience of believers must be based on what God's word says. Every revealed truth must be received with faith and love. Even those truths for which we cannot discern any immediate use in our communion with God should be accepted because all truth is from God.

Scripture is a revelation of God's will and grace. The whole trend of scripture is to bring us into a conformity with God. "All scripture is God-breathed and is useful . . . for training in righteousness, so that the man of God may be thoroughly equipped for every good work" (II Timothy 3:16,17). Paul in Titus 1:1 speaks of the knowledge of the truth that leads to godliness. The word that is according to godliness, the revealed will of God, leads to our sanctification (I Thessalonians 4:3-5). The scriptures are the instrument by which God produces our holiness, as Jesus said: "Sanctify them by the truth; your word is truth" (John 17:17). Every gospel truth has the effect spoken of in II Corinthians 3:18: "We, who with unveiled faces all reflect the Lord's glory, are being transformed into his likeness with ever-increasing glory, which comes from the Lord, who is the Spirit". Unless this happens in our lives, we have not received the truth of the gospel. Paul makes it very clear in Titus 2:11,12 that whatever men may claim for themselves, "the grace of God . . . teaches us to say 'no' to ungodliness and worldly passions and to live self-controlled, upright and godly lives in this present age". We must recognise that some truths promote holiness more strongly than others. This is specially true of the love of Christ. In II Corinthians 5:14 Christ's love is said to constrain or compel us. Other truths may persuade, and do so effectively, but it is the love of Christ which compels. Great emphasis is laid in scripture on those doctrines which bring about holiness of heart and which lead to faith, love and reverence for God. Believers are called to glorify God in these ways.

We need to be guided by what the scriptures have to say about the truths that lead to godliness rather than depend on the wisdom of men. Men's opinions vary so greatly that we can never be sure that they are reliable. We can argue that if acceptance of a particular truth encourages holiness, then it should be greatly prized. Another argument is that if a certain line of teaching leads us to greater godliness, it must be truth. But this could be a dangerous assumption. Any teaching which has no other proof of its worth to make us holy than men's opinions of it, we should reject. We must look more closely at what the scriptures mean by obedience to the gospel.

We can perhaps define it quite simply as a willing subjection of oneself, in an orderly way, to the whole will of God. David recognised this when he declared:

"To do your will, O my God, is my desire; your law is within my heart" (Psalm 40:8). The apostle Paul calls the believers at Rome to practise this subjection to the will of God. He says: "I urge you, brothers, in view of God's mercy, to offer your bodies as living sacrifices, holy and pleasing to God – which is your spiritual worship. Do not conform any longer to the pattern of this world, but be transformed by the renewing of your mind" (Romans 12:1,2). Obedience to the gospel does not differ essentially from what God's law requires but its underlying principles and its purpose belong only to the gospel.

We will consider four aspects of obedience to the gospel:

1. Its nature
2. The cause of it in us
3. Its motives
4. Those who are obedient

Our aim in doing this is to show that the doctrine of the perseverance of believers really does lead to obedience, even though there are those who would claim that it has the opposite effect.

1. Obedience is doing all those things, and only those things, that God commands. There are inward acts of obedience which spring from faith and love. There are also outward acts of religious duties which God has told us to do. All that we start to do as Christians, and what we continue to do, must be based on faith, for "without faith it is impossible to please God" (Hebrews 11:6). Paul, in Romans 1:5, speaks of the obedience that comes from faith because Christ dwells in our hearts through faith (Ephesians 3:17). In fact, as Jesus said: "Apart from me you can do nothing" (John 15:5). The chief outcome of our obedience is the glory of God who rewards not according to our deeds but according to the freeness of his grace and mercy.

2. *What other cause is there of Christian obedience?* In every born-again believer, two opposing principles are at work – flesh and spirit; the old nature and the new nature; indwelling sin and grace. The Spirit and he alone gives rise to obedience. Those who are new creations in Christ Jesus are strengthened with might by his Spirit (Ephesians 3:16-19). Because the Spirit lives in them their faith, love and knowledge increase. The opposing principle – the flesh – leads only to deeds of the flesh, as Jesus told Nicodemus: "Flesh gives birth to flesh" (John 3:6). We might ask: "Is it possible for obedience ever to be abominable to the Lord?" Yes it can be, if it springs merely from selfishness and fear of punishment (II Kings 17:25,32-34).

3. *What then are the motives that should govern Christian obedience?* They must produce faith and love to God, drawing the believer closer to God. As the believer increasingly understands the truth of the gospel, so obedience grows. The grace of God in us has the effect of subduing sin in our lives. The love of Christ shown in his death on the cross is a truth which leads to obedience. The law humbles a person for Christ while the gospel humbles a person in Christ. In Romans 6 Paul shows in what way the body of sin is to be put to death. He demonstrates the folly of trying to establish our own righteousness by resorting to deeds of the flesh such as self-inflicted sufferings. Those who do this have no understanding of what the righteousness of God means.

4. *Who are those who are inspired by the doctrine of the perseverance of believers to holiness and obedience?* Those

who really believe it! They are taught by God not to turn the grace of God into an excuse for sin. The knowledge that the love of God to believers cannot alter is a powerful motive to obedience even though unbelievers may challenge it. All discouragements are removed and everything that would weaken their faith in God. They are set at perfect liberty through Christ. All that would make their obedience unacceptable to God is swept away.

A Christian who relies on his own efforts instead of on the love and faithfulness of God to preserve him cannot know peace. He may remember that the angels who fell once knew the joys of heaven though now they are for ever confined to hell. It would be no comfort to remember that Adam did not persevere in paradise even though in his original state he had no indwelling sin to lure him into temptation. Would not such a Christian cry out: "Is there no promise of God I can rest on, or prayer of Christ I can cling to?"

Hard thoughts against God which weaken our love for him cannot long be entertained when we consider God's love for us. This is well expressed in Zephaniah 3:17: "The Lord your God is with you, he is mighty to save. He will take great delight in you. He will quiet you with his love. He will rejoice over you with singing".

God's people, who have been assured in this way of his love for them and who have been made alive by his Spirit, are laid under an obligation always to be "perfecting holiness out of reverence for God" (II Corinthians 7:1). Can it be supposed that those whom God has called heirs of heaven and glory are prepared to give themselves over to wickedness of all kinds because they know that God's love for them is

69

unchangeable? Is it conceivable that the people of God, knowing that he loves them with an everlasting love, should then proceed to hate him?

Those who object to the doctrine of the perseverance of believers sometimes claim that it takes away the restraining the flesh needs from fear of hell and punishment to bring about obedience. But the flesh with all its deeds must be put to death. The apostle has a short answer to any who say: "Let us continue in sin because we are not under its condemnation but under grace". His answer is an emphatic denial, "No!" (Romans 6:2).

What is meant by putting the flesh to death? Romans 8:3 says: "If by the Spirit you put to death the misdeeds of the body, you will live". So it is by the Spirit that believers do this and not because of fear of hell and punishment. Many have tried by their own efforts to kill their bodily desires but have never once succeeded. Law-keeping cannot do more than restrain sin. It can never abolish it. What then does the Spirit use to put to death our sinful nature? He uses what Christ accomplished by his death on the cross and his love shown then. This brings about the true death of sin in the believer. "By the cross of Christ the world has been crucified to me and I to the world" (Galatians 6:14). The constraining love of Christ ensures "that those who live should no longer live for themselves but for him who died for them and was raised again" (II Corinthians 5:15).

Faith in God and in Jesus Christ, the basis of all the believers' obedience, is strengthened by an assurance that they will persevere. The discovery of God's good will towards them increases their faith in God as Father and in the Lord Jesus Christ as Mediator. They know that God who begins the good work in them will perfect it in the day of Jesus Christ. The one who gave his people new life when they were dead in trespasses and sins is the one who will keep them to the end, in spite of Satan's powerful temptations and the sinfulness of their own hearts.

When God makes his love known to us, our faith is strengthened and our love for him grows. "We love him because he first loved us" (I John 4:19). The terror of the Lord causes us to persuade others but the love of Christ persuades us to live for him. She loved much to whom much was forgiven.

The perseverance of the saints demonstrates the glory of the love of God. This love has three characteristics which ensure the perseverance of believers:

1. freedom
2. unchangeableness
3. fruitfulness

1. The freedom of God's love. God first loved his people not because they were better than others but because of his grace. He continues his love to them not on the condition that they reach a certain level of holiness but in order that they shall be holy. Who can resist the love of God? Our response to God's love is to love him in return and to obey him.

2. The unchangeableness of God's love. We have seen before the constancy of God's love. In Zephaniah 3:17 God is said to rest in his love. Surely it dishonours God to claim that he can love his people one day and hate them the next? Could he rejoice over them one day and on another cast them into hell? Though people cannot always be sure how those whom they love will act, this can never be true of God, "before whom all things are naked and open". Some might say that people change from what they were when God first loved them, so his love also changes. But we ask: "What caused them to be loved in the first place?" Was it not the Lord? Did they make themselves different from others? Did he not love them because of his own grace? Is not he that set his love on them in the first place able to keep them in the state of being loved? If he determined not to preserve them in his love, why did he love them at the first? The certainty of the unchangeableness of the love of God is so precious to his people.

3. *The fruitfulness of God's love.* The love of a mother for her children will cause her to sacrifice everything for their protection. In a much greater way God will use his mighty power for the preservation of his saints. We see that the doctrine of their perseverance gives the love of God glory because of its fruitfulness. Because he loves with an everlasting love, therefore with lovingkindness he draws us (Jeremiah 31:3). From that love flow such continual supplies of his Spirit and grace that his people will lack nothing (Psalm 23:1). Can we who have been so blessed resist the gracious influences he brings to bear upon us? Christ becomes very precious to us. By his death we have peace with God for he has obtained eternal redemption for us and ended all controversy between God and us. He did not suffer so much for us for an uncertain end, depending on whether we accept or reject him as our sinful nature may decide. Rather he will without fail bring to God those for whom he died and justify, sanctify and preserve them by his Spirit and his grace.

11.
Consideration of passages of Scripture sometimes used against final perseverance

In this final chapter we will consider certain texts of scripture which some people have twisted to prove to their own satisfaction the possibility of the apostasy of saints. Some people say that if God graciously forgives sin, they can live immoral lives. The gospel becomes the "smell of death" to such. It is the "fragrance of life" to those who wholeheartedly receive it and obey it.

Paul emphasises that it is God's will that every believer should be holy (I Thessalonians 4:3). Any teaching which turns people away from walking with God is not from God but from the evil one. Nevertheless, even these so-called Christian teachers will not admit that their teaching is the cause of unholy living. There are some who have built up systems of human merits, penances and the like, in the place of the merits of Christ. Paul says that such rules "indeed have an appearance of wisdom with their self-imposed worship and their harsh treatment of the body, but they lack any value in restraining sensual indulgence" (Colossians 2:23).

If people do not know what true holiness is, how can they judge what doctrines really promote it? What can we say about anyone who thinks he has power in himself to yield to God the obedience required? What about the person who thinks that threats of hell are the most powerful motives for obedience? Every true Christian will know that the grace of God is necessary if he is to do good. The judgment of those who are not true believers must be seriously questioned. They cannot decide whether a certain teaching leads to godliness or not.

There are many opinions about the nature of godliness. What guidance can be offered to anyone wanting to know what encourages it most? We can safely say that every gospel truth encourages those who receive it to obey it. The doctrine of the perseverance of believers does promote godliness in their lives. We must find out what the scriptures say on this subject. The promises in the scripture concerning guidance direct us in a sure way.

There have been many instances of people who gave the appearance of being true believers by their clean lives. They hear biblical truth gladly, as Herod did; accept it with joy, as did the stony ground; and receive it, like those spoken of in Ezekiel 33:31: "My people come to you as they usually do and sit before you to listen to your words, but they do not put them into practice. With their mouths they express devotion but their hearts are greedy for unjust gain". Many of these people may, as Judas was, be thought of by others for a time as true believers and yet never have been saved by Jesus Christ.

Some people have used certain scriptures to claim the possibility of the apostasy of believers. One such scripture is Ezekiel 18:24,25: "But if a righteous man turns from his righteousness and commits sin and does the same detestable things as the wicked man does, will he live? None of the righteous things he has done will be remembered. Because of the unfaithfulness he is guilty of and because of the sin he has committed he will die". These words describe a controversy at a particular time in Israel's history between God and the Jews concerning their use of the proverb given in verse 2 and 3 of that chapter. "The fathers eat sour grapes and the children's teeth are set on edge". The word of the Lord given as an answer in verses 24 and 25 is intended to disprove the general application of the proverb. The statement cannot be taken as establishing the way God acts in dealing with his people. The proverb is about the land of Israel, as verse 2 clearly states. That land had been given to the nation of the Jews until they were carried off to Babylon as captives because of their obstinate wickedness. By that captivity God repaid to them not only the sins of that generation but those of their forefathers, particularly Manasseh. They had invented the proverb while in captivity in self-justification. God, in his reply, vindicated the justice of his dealings with them. Everyone of them had suffered because of his own sin. There is no analogy here between God's dealings with Israel in regard to the land of Canaan and his dealings with the church today. In fact, there is a great contrast between the principle laid down in verse 4: "The soul who sins is the one who will die" and that of God's grace in sending his Son as an atoning sacrifice for his people.

In case anyone should still think that the passage in Ezekiel 18 lends support to any likelihood of the apostasy of saints, let us examine it more closely. We note first that the expression raises only a possibility – "if". It is a hypothetical statement. The words are: "If a righteous man turns from his righteousness and commits sin . . . he will die" (verse 24). Some people have interpreted it this way: God is merely stating what sin deserves and the inevitable connection between apostasy and punishment. This does not prove that anyone who is truly righteous will fall away from God for ever. Indeed, they say, God actually used these warnings to keep believers from apostasy. There is a connection between turning away and dying; but to conclude that a righteous man will so fall away is to go beyond anything the text says. Against this, other people have held the view that conditional sayings which include promises and threats do at least suppose a possibility, even though the condition is never actually met. Of course, a possibility can be prevented from happening by the intervention of the Spirit and the grace of God.

We must look in greater detail at what is meant by "a righteous man". The context of Ezekiel 18 strongly indicates that it means a man who keeps the commandments of God given in the Old Testament. Through this covenant the people retained possession of the land and future spiritual events were typified.

Some people have suggested that the righteous man referred to by Ezekiel is righteous in appearance only. This view seems contrary to the whole idea of the passage, so other people say that many people do try sincerely to obey the laws of God. They are able, to some degree, to obey God's commands. They may be said to be righteous and certainly are so compared with those who openly rebel against God. Such righteousness is rewarded by God in this life, especially in Old Testament days. Yet upright people, doing all known religious duties, may not be members of God's spiritual family. They are not built on the rock Christ Jesus and many of them do fall into grievous sins and come under the judgment of God. Their righteousness, though sincere, falls short of the righteousness which comes through faith in Christ which alone is acceptable to God.

There can be no doubt that the wicked man spoken of in Ezekiel 18 does not merely seem to be wicked but is actually so. In a parallel way, it may justly be claimed that the righteous man spoken of is truly righteous with the kind of righteouness intended in the context. Should he continue to be righteous he would receive the reward spoken of in the chapter. Perhaps he is a Christian but nothing in the verses indicates that that is definitely the case.

Another interpretation has been put forward which has some support from the scriptures. This is that there is a double righteousness – one, of works, by which we are sanctified; the other, of faith, by which we are justified. A righteous man may stop living a holy life but it does not follow that he has lost the righteousness of Christ. This interpretation does not claim that sanctification and justification can exist completely independently of each other in a believer, for "without holiness no-one will see the Lord" (Hebrews 12:14). But a person can fall away from the righteousness of sanctification in two ways: first, from the practice of it, and second, from the principle of it. It is sadly true that a person may, under strong temptation, cease from practising holiness until he no longer produces spiritual fruit. This may lead to severe chastening from the Lord in his life and even death, as in the case of Josiah. And second, no-one who once holds the principles of holiness can ever completely forsake them. So we see that a justified and sanctified person may for a time depart from holiness and provoke the Lord to deal sharply, even terribly, with him. Yet such a person does not lose his relationship to Christ nor forfeit God's love for him.

77

All who are saved are justified in God's sight. Yet the consciousness of our justification and the peace and comfort it brings are subject to increases and decreases. Justified and sanctified persons can so drift away from a close walk with God that, like a tree in winter, they cease to bring forth fruits of holiness. They can lose their sense of acceptance with God through Christ and the peace that goes with it but they cannot wholly be cast out of the favour of God. Some people have argued that the death spoken of in Ezekiel 18 can only mean eternal death but that is not proved by the passage in question. In a similar way, we could not say that all the Israelites who died in the wilderness because of their sins went to hell.

Let us turn to another scripture on which some have based a claim that the saints of God may become unbelievers. This is the sequel to the Lord's parable of the unmerciful servant in Matthew 18:21-35. It is argued that the parable was addressed to the disciples, and to Peter in particular, of whom there can be no doubt that he was truly born again and justified before God. Yet the Lord plainly states that unless they freely forgive those who sin against them they will not be forgiven by the Father.

To interpret this parable, as some have done, to make it teach that believers may because of their sins perish eternally, is not reasonable. The plain teaching of the parable is surely that because people have received mercy and forgiveness from God in Christ they, in turn, ought to show mercy and kindness to others. To say this in another way – we have no right to expect God graciously to forgive those who show no compassion to other people.

A third scripture which is sometimes quoted to try to prove the possibility of the apostasy of believers is I

Corinthians 9:27. Here Paul speaks of his concern that despite his conversion and having preached to others, he would in the end be disqualified. We have earlier shown that God's appointed means of attaining a declared end should be properly used. Our Saviour used the ordinary means of preserving his life even though he had the promise of being kept by the angels. Hezekiah, too, took food and drink though God had promised an extension of 15 years to his life. Paul also was careful to look after himself. Paul was concerned that having preaching the gospel as his main aim, he should through personal holiness and self-denial ensure that the work was not hindered by his elation at the revelations made to him. His great concern was that he should be a "workman needing not to be ashamed", not only preaching to others for their good but being himself approved by God. He recognised that his work could continue and yet he himself not be approved in the work and so lose his reward. To interpret the Greek word used in this passage to mean a man finally rejected by God is to go beyond its legitimate meaning both in this context and elsewhere in scripture. The apostle, aware that he was sent by the Lord to preach the gospel, also greatly valued Christ's commendation. He would not spare himself in order faithfully to fulfil his ministry.

Hebrews 6:4-8 and 10:26-39 are other scriptures which some have used seriously to question the perseverance of believers. The word of God through the Holy Spirit does bring about a marked change in the life of many who are not truly born again. Such persons may sincerely agree to the truth and live lives consistent with their grasp of it. They cannot be said to be hypocrites. Nevertheless, because they seek a righteousness through the works of the law, the righteousness of Christ proves to have no effect in their lives. Many like this scrupulously avoid sin in their lives and often have gifts which can serve the church. To apostatise from such a standard is dangerous and may lead to sin against the Holy Spirit. Note that in the passage which speaks of such people there is no mention of the special characteristics of true believers. They are not said to have living faith in them nor are they described as having the faith of God's elect. They are not said to be justified, united to Christ, sanctified by the Spirit, and the things which accompany salvation are not said to be evident in their lives. In contrast, when the apostle in chapter six speaks of true believers he speaks of their work and love (verse 10), the unchanging nature of his purpose and his oath for their preservation (verse 17). We must conclude therefore that those about whom the apostle writes with such solemn warnings are not the justified and sanctified children of God.

Some people have attempted to prove that the apostle speaks merely of hypocrites but that is clearly not his intention. On the contrary, he is showing how like true believers they may be and yet fall away into sin. They do not fall away from their hypocrisy but from this profession of the faith and from the gifts of common grace they once enjoyed.

In Hebrews 6:4 the apostle speaks of those who have once been enlightened. It is certain that true believers have been "enlightened" but the word is capable of more than one meaning. Those spoken of in this verse are also said to have been "enlightened", but to argue from this that they are therefore true believers is false logic. Similar considerations apply in the case of Hebrews 10:26: "after we have received the knowledge of the truth". People may be so convinced by the word

80

of God as sincerely to acknowledge the truth of the gospel and yet come short of that real union with Christ which all true believers have.

In Hebrews 10:29 the apostle describes one who "has treated as an unholy thing the blood of the covenant that sanctified him". People may be so convicted by the preaching of the cross and the shedding of the blood of Christ that they readily separate themselves from those who reject biblical teaching. They may, however, be far from having "consciences cleansed from dead works to serve the living God". In the scriptures, the word "sanctifying" has two distinct meanings. First, it means to separate, to set apart, to God. The Old Testament uses it mainly to describe inanimate objects. Second, it means to purify, to cleanse with a spiritual purity – the opposite of being defiled by sin. With this meaning, it is used mainly of persons. In the Epistle to the Hebrews, where the apostle uses many terms belonging to the old worship, the word is almost always used in the first sense and also in John 17:19 where the Saviour speaks of dedicating himself to his work as our great high priest. We have earlier shown that many consider themselves sanctified in the second sense who were never truly cleansed from their sins.

There are those who are said to have "tasted the heavenly gift" (Hebrews 6:4). Without discussing the true nature of the "heavenly gift", we note that these people are said only to taste it. They do not feed on it or grow by doing so. People by the preaching of the word may become troubled in their consciences and forced to look for help. If they have come to some (though small) appreciation of the answer provided for sinners in Jesus Christ, but then reject it, they are guilty of a terrible undervaluing of Christ and the love of God. By their renunciation of Christ they openly declare that they have not found in him the real goodness and excellency that some claim to have found. God must judge them accordingly.

Those spoken of in Hebrews 6:4 are also said to have "shared in the Holy Spirit". The Holy Spirit's gifts or graces are meant. We have earlier showed that those who have been born again, made alive to God, sealed and comforted by the Holy Spirit, can never lose him. They enjoy God's love and favour now and will finally reach the full enjoyment of the glory he has provided for them. Certainly as far as gifts are concerned there are many who excel in these and yet never show that faith which gives real union with Jesus Christ.

We now consider Hebrews 10:38: "Now the just shall live by faith: but if any man draw back, my soul shall have no pleasure in him". In the earlier part of this chapter the apostle is considering two kinds of people. 1. Those who had given up meeting together, withdrawn from the church and gradually backslidden. 2. Those who continued in spite of persecutions to hold fast their confidence so that they might receive the promised reward. To these he repeats the promise given to Habakkuk – "The just shall live by faith". The apostle was certain that they would continue to believe and be saved. Some others drew back to their destruction but they never were true believers, whatever their gifts and attainments.

We continue by examining the parable of the four soils, especially that part which deals with the stony ground in Matthew 13:20,21. The seed in rocky places represents the man who hears the word and at once receives it with joy. But since he has no root he lasts only a short time and quickly withers. Claims have been made that the stony ground hearers are true believers but it is hard to recognise saving faith in them. A faith which totally lacks root, fruit or continuance can hardly be described as saving faith. They are like Herod who heard the word gladly. We say again that details of the parables should not be pressed beyond the plain meaning of the parable. Our Lord's intention here is clearly to show that many hear the word of the gospel in vain and bring forth no fruit at all. What really matters is fruit-bearing. The absence of true fruit-bearing shows they were never true believers. A faith which does not produce works acceptable to God is dead.

In conclusion we turn to II Peter 2:18-22 as the last of the scriptures we shall consider in this way which have been used to discredit the doctrine of the perseverance of saints. Meeting as we do many who answer to this description, we see little resemblance in them to any who have faith in Jesus Christ. We admit that there are those who through the faithful preaching of the word are affected by it. Acknowledging the truth and the power of the word of God they reform their conduct but are not changed in heart. Some in due course return to their ungodly ways, though others continue to the end in their renewed manner of life. Paul describes such in II Timothy 3:5 as "having a form of godliness but denying its power". They are not hypocrites pretending to be what they are not and hiding all kinds of vices under a cloak of religion. We have seen previously how it is possible for people to "walk conscientiously", as Paul did before his conversion, and yet not be members of Christ's family. They may fairly be said to have escaped from those who live in error and yet may never be true believers born again of the Holy Spirit. As we have seen many times in our consideration of this doctrine God uses these cautions as means by which his people are preserved to eternal life. The warnings of scripture are not inconsistent with God's infallible promises concerning the perseverance of his saints and are part of God's dealings with believers to keep them living obediently with him.

GREAT CHRISTIAN CLASSICS

'Many pastors and counsellors have wished for readable modern versions of Protestant classics. The Great Christian Classics series seeks to meet the need. These books are abridged and simplified versions of some of the greatest practical theology books ever written. They are also inexpensive!'

(The Journal of Biblical Counselling — 1996)

Titles available from
Grace Publications

No. 1 LIFE BY HIS DEATH
Prepared by H. J. Appleby
John Owen's **The Death of Death in the Death of Christ**
Paperback, 87 pages. ISBN 0 9505476 3 8

No. 2 GOD WILLING
Prepared by H. Mockford
John Flavel's **Divine Conduct or The Mystery of Providence**
Paperback, 65 pages. ISBN 0 9505476 6 2

No. 3 BIBLICAL CHRISTIANITY
Prepared by B. R. Woods
John Calvin's **The Institutes of the Christian Religion**
Paperback, 125 pages. ISBN 0 9505476 7 0

No. 4 BY GOD'S GRACE ALONE
Prepared by H. J. Appleby
Abraham Booth's **The Reign of Grace**
Paperback, 73 pages. ISBN 0 946462 01 1

No. 5   BORN SLAVES
Prepared by Clifford Pond
Martin Luther's **The Bondage of the Will**
Paperback, 93 pages. ISBN 0 946462 02 X

No. 6   THE GLORY OF CHRIST
Prepared by H. Mockford
John Owen's **The Glory of Christ**
Paperback, 86 pages. ISBN 0 946462 13 5

No. 7   CHRISTIANS ARE FOR EVER
Prepared by H. Lawrence
John Owen's **The Perseverance of the Saints**
Paperback, 84 pages. ISBN 0 946462 14 3

No. 8   THINKING SPIRITUALLY
John Owen's **The Grace and Duty of being Spiritually Minded**
Paperback, 95 pages. ISBN 0 946462 21 6

No. 9   LEARNING TO BE HAPPY
Jeremiah Burrough's **The Rare jewel of Christian Contentment**
Paperback, 80 pages. ISBN 0 946462 16 X

SPECIAL CHILDREN?
A theology of childhood

Eric Lane
This is a book for Christian parents who want to know
what the Bible has to say about their children. It deals
with many of the questions that parents raise concerning the spiritual standing of their children.
Paperback, 160 pages. ISBN 0 946462 39 9

THE BEAUTY OF JESUS

Clifford Pond
A refreshing portrait of the perfect human character of
Jesus Christ that takes us to the heart of the Christian
faith and of Christian experience.
Paperback, 144 pages. ISBN 0 946462 33 X

OUR FATHER
Enjoying the Fatherhood of God!

Clifford Pond
This book sets out to establish that the fatherhood of
God is not only a doctrine to be believed and defended,
it is a relationship into which every believer enters and
which every believer is intended to enjoy.
Paperback, 112 pages. ISBN 0 946462 43 7

DICTIONARY OF BIBLE SYMBOLS

A dictionary of the 'pictures' or figurative use of
language in the Bible.
Paperback, 176 pages. ISBN 0 946462 27 5

DICTIONARY OF THEOLOGICAL
TERMS

M. E. Manton
Theological terms are explained in clear and succinct
definitions, designed to be helpful in understanding the
technical 'framework' of Christianity.
Paperback, 112 pages. ISBN 0 946462 40 2

DICTIONARY OF BIBLE KNOWLEDGE

I. Stringer
Clearly written explanatory paragraphs on almost 400
biblical topics in non-technical language.
Paperback, 208 pages. ISBN 0 946462 41 0

THE REAL THING?

Philip Tait
A contemporary and abridged form of Gardiner
Spring's *Distinguishing traits of Christian character*,
first published in 1829.
Evangelistic Booklet, 48 pages. ISBN 0 946462 30 5

...TO TELL THE TRUTH
**Some biblical guidelines to help Christians talk
about the Faith**

John Appleby
An introduction to Christian communication that is
faithful to Scripture and will challenge the readers to a
boldness in moving out from the sub-culture of the
church and taking the Word of life into the world.
Paperback, 144 pages. ISBN 0 946462 42 9

**Distributed by Evangelical Press
12 Wooler Street
Darlington
Co. Durham
DL1 1RQ**